Jazz Fest
MEMORIES

Miles Davis, 1985.

Jazz Fest
MEMORIES

By Michael P. Smith and Allison Miner

Foreword by
Quint Davis

PELICAN PUBLISHING COMPANY
Gretna 1997

*The word "Pelican" and the depiction of a pelican are trademarks
of Pelican Publishing Company, Inc.,
and are registered in the U.S. Patent and Trademark Office.*

Library of Congress Cataloging-in-Publication Data

Miner, Allison, 1949-1995.
    Jazz fest memories / Allison Miner ; photographs by Michael P.
Smith ; foreword by Quint Davis.
       p.   cm.
     ISBN 1-56554-157-X (pbk.)
     1. New Orleans Jazz & Heritage Festival. 2. Jazz—Louisiana—New
Orleans—History and criticism. I. Smith, Michael P. (Michael
Procter), 1937- . II. Title.
ML38.N28N4 1997
781.65'079'76335—dc21   96-47438
                                             CIP
                                             MN

The New Orleans Jazz & Heritage Festival is staged annually by the
New Orleans Jazz & Heritage Foundation, Inc., a nonprofit corpo-
ration dedicated to this purpose and to preserving and fostering the
rich music and cultural heritage of New Orleans and Louisiana.
The publisher acknowledges that the marks of "Jazz Fest" and "New
Orleans Jazz Festival" are registered marks of the New Orleans Jazz
& Heritage Foundation, Inc.

Printed in China

Published by Pelican Publishing Company, Inc.
1101 Monroe Street, Gretna, Louisiana 70053

To New Orleans jazz and heritage

The two "grand marshals" Anderson Minor and Matthew ("Fats") Houston (1973) were the last of the truly serious marshals. They walked the streets of New Orleans with various brass bands, for miles and miles and on all occasions, bringing great dignity to the task.

Contents

"Deacon John" Moore, 1995.

Foreword

Editor's Note: Allison Miner, one of the founders of the New Orleans Jazz & Heritage Festival, died of multiple myeloma (bone-marrow cancer) on December 23, 1995. She was an extraordinary woman and is missed by music lovers all around the world. Her memories of the festival are an important part of New Orleans history.

She would be awakened at three o'clock in the morning by a phone call from anywhere in the world: "Allison, the equipment is lost; the bus driver was arrested; the rental car had a flat; we can't find the hotel; your credit card, your mom's credit card, and that loan on the house mortgage are all canceled; we didn't get paid last night; the bass player quit; and someone threw up on the queen at the state dinner."

And after she got through dealing with it all, she would always set her jaw, shake her head, look toward the heavens, and say, "God love 'em!" Whether it was Professor Longhair or Tuts Washington or the Wild Magnolias or Re-Birth Brass Band or whomever, "God love 'em" because they were earthly communicators of the soul; they were music makers. This, of course, was a self-fulfilling prophecy, because Allison saying, "God love 'em," about one of the groups she was working with was proof that He did, by sending this angel to earth to care for them.

For Allison was one of those saint people who actually cared more for the well-being of others than her own. No one who worked with her will find that again.

Allison stressed the connection between music and the people who make it. If you listen to, feel, and love the music, you must always follow it to its source and come to know and define it by the person who made it. And with this inseparability comes a responsibility. You may not have this music unjustly; you must look the music maker in the eye and know that he or she has been treated fairly, paid fairly, gotten his or her royalty, and gotten his or her publishing. For this beautiful gift that they were fated to give the world, these heavenly music makers cannot be left behind. This is the lesson I believe she lived for and the work and consciousness she left for us to carry on.

Allison's ultimate gift to the Jazz & Heritage Festival was that it was to be about the musicians first, that its focus and identity and texture come from the humanity of the musicians themselves, as people, who define this culture through their gift of song. Fess, Clifton Chenier, James Booker, James Black, Danny Barker, Kid Thomas, Mahalia Jackson, Muddy Waters, Miles Davis, Charles Mingus, Percy and Willie Humphrey, Chief Jolly and Jumper, the Balfas, Rockin' Dopsie, Bukka White, Roosevelt Sykes, Lightnin' Hopkins, and Robert Pete Williams—she made sure that truly to know and love their music, we must know and love *them*.

Thank you, Allison, really, thank you for everything.

QUINT DAVIS

Young Men Olympian Social & Pleasure Club, 1983.

Introduction

Allison Miner came to New Orleans not looking for a job, but looking for a life . . . and she found her life in nourishing our culture and music. Allison's spirit was full of song and dance, and in this city she found the right soil in which to grow and blossom.

Allison quickly found her way to the Jazz Archives at Tulane University, where she was an invaluable worker, helping to preserve our city's music heritage. I didn't get to know Allison well, though, and deeply respect her, until I found her out in the streets, again and again, following traditional African-American social and pleasure club parades, Mardi Gras Indian marches, and jazz funerals. More important, she was also at their "practices," dinners, dances, birthday parties, picnics, and all kinds of other special occasions. Allison followed music and culture in New Orleans to their most profound roots. She not only understood the cultural dynamics that generated and sustained our traditional music, but she also went to where the real music was—the small neighborhood clubs and the street parades. In doing so she gave to it, and became a part of it, literally. She joined the drummers in the "second-line" processions, playing a Cajun triangle.

Soon Allison joined Quint Davis and George Wein in founding the New Orleans Jazz & Heritage Festival. She also managed Professor Longhair and was instrumental in promoting and directing the careers of other great musicians—the Wild Magnolias, the Golden Eagles, Eddie Bo, Re-Birth, Willie and Earl Turbinton, to mention just a few. Allison's intelligence, heartfelt knowledge of traditional music, generous care and fair treatment of the musicians who performed at the Jazz Fest, and other work in establishing and managing the festival during its early years set a high standard and will never be forgotten. It was because of her deep involvement in New Orleans music that I asked her to share her memories in this book.

11

JAZZ FEST MEMORIES

I apologize to the reader for my lack of color documentation in the early years of the festival. At that time, I had little money to shoot in color and I was convinced that black and white was the best choice for historical purposes. Some of the individuals mentioned herein are not pictured, but many are well represented in black and white in *New Orleans Jazz Fest: A Pictorial History* and *A Joyful Noise: A Celebration of New Orleans Music* (both available from Pelican Publishing Company). Those books make up the definitive part of my festival collection, but the color work that *Jazz Fest Memories* presents is certainly "the icing on the cake." This is the first time I've looked at much of this color work and I'm glad it is now preserved in a relatively permanent form for everybody to review and enjoy.

Documenting the evolution of the New Orleans Jazz Festival has been a very special pleasure because of the vast and diverse collection of regional food, folk arts and crafts, and music it presents. For me, more important than anything else, the Jazz Festival has proved that our unique cultural recreations in New Orleans are a gigantic economic and social resource for the city. It shouldn't go unnoticed that our festival is renowned as the safest event of its size on earth. And I would add that such a festival, presenting traditional food, music, arts, crafts, and dance, goes far beyond simple entertainment; all together it is recreation of the highest order, a religious experience that fills the soul.

The New Orleans Jazz Fest has grown to be the most important event of its type in the world. We are pleased to share some of these colorful "growing-up" years with a wider public. We hope you will visit or revisit this wonderful event in person in years to come.

Allison's tragic death occurred before we completed work on this book. Fortunately, her "memories" were tape-recorded by Clare Beth Pierson, a very special friend who was concerned about Allison's ability to conclude her part of the text. Given her bone-marrow transplant, chemotherapy, and other ongoing treatments for her cancer, Allison had little energy to continue her numerous endeavors. We are in great debt to Clare Pierson for organizing, editing, and refining the many hours of recordings that she collected for presentation here. The complete recordings of Allison's Jazz Fest memories and all the photographs in this book will become a part of the permanent collection of the New Orleans Jazz & Heritage Foundation Archives. Allison's charge there is now being carried forward by Monifa Johnson.

MICHAEL P. SMITH

Born on September 23, 1949 to a family who listened to and appreciated traditional jazz as well as country tunes and gospel, Allison Miner grew up with music in her heart and soul. Her school book reports were always about women whose names are synonymous with the blues, singers like Bessie Smith and Billie Holiday; and her high-school peers were Greg and Duane Allman, whose musical group was first known as A. Miner and the Allman Joys.

Allison came to the Crescent City in 1967. It was the summer of love, the beginning of the psychedelic era. Both Allison and Quint Davis, a young musician, worked for Dick Allen as archivists at the William R. Hogan Archives of New Orleans Jazz at Tulane University. It was a chance phone call to Dick that led both Allison and Quint to George Wein, a jazz aficionado who had an idea about starting a music festival in New Orleans. Allison and Quint were not only interested, they were willing to provide the brain power and the energy to do whatever was necessary to run with the dream and make it the reality it is today.

Working together, they selected and secured the musicians who would perform and then made sure they were treated well, with love and respect. They opened their homes and their hearts to feed and shelter music greats like Robert Pete Williams, Bukka White, and Big Joe Williams during the festival. It was always important to Allison that the musicians enjoy the festival and remember it happily. She touched people's lives with her affection and generous spirit. She continued that tradition through her early years with the festival and later with her Music Heritage Interviews. Talking to Allison was natural because she was genuinely interested in the oral history of the music as well as the musicians.

During the next several years, Allison's talent for development became more personal: she married and had her two sons, Jonathan, in 1978, and Rashi, in 1980. Whenever she was asked about her many accomplishments and honors she had received, she said that her greatest legacy was her children and that nothing else she had ever done meant more to her than they did.

While away from New Orleans, Allison continued to coordinate and direct various music projects, including a Summer Arts Festival in Ohio and a Folk Life Festival for the Smithsonian Institution in Washington, D.C. She served on many advisory boards, such as for the Case Western Reserve University radio station (WRUW) and the Northeast Ohio Jazz Society.

Allison's creativity manifested itself in many ways. She was programming coordinator for the Folk Life Pavilion at the 1984 Louisiana World Exposition. She directed the Contemporary Arts Center's Jazz Factory, an organization that later evolved into the Louisiana Jazz Federation, a group responsible for devising a program that put jazz into the public-school system. For her pivotal role in this development, Allison was the 1994 recipient of the Jazz Town Award. She was honored by the Contemporary Arts Center as a SweetArt and also received the prestigious Mayor's Arts Award given by the Arts Council of New Orleans. It will not be the great distinctions or the distinguised citations for which Allison will be remembered; rather it will be her sensitivity to the music she heard.

Two of Allison's most valuable contributions to the music world have been the establishment of the New Orleans Jazz & Heritage Festival Foundation Archives and her interviews with musicians from all over the world who were appearing at the Jazz Festival. Allison returned to the festival staff in 1988 as coordinator of the Music Heritage Stage, a position she created because she understood the importance of respecting the cultures and preserving the histories of these talented men and women. Allison and her assistant collected hundreds of hours of conversations, which record the past and document the present. Allison worked very hard at perfecting this skill, which quickly became an art in her caring and capable hands. Her lyrical facility with language and her inquisitive yet comforting style of expression encouraged people to talk easily and naturally about their music and themselves.

Allison Miner played a very large part in offering millions of people from all over the world the opportunity to listen and be transformed, to become better people by moving away from the daily routine and being lifted up by the music she loved.

For the last three years of her life Allison had been battling a debilitating and deadly bone-marrow cancer, multiple myeloma. She had already undergone one bone-marrow transplant and was awaiting another when I was asked to help with the book. In a series of interviews, we talked into a tape recorder that she was particularly proud of: she had purchased it with the first money she earned from the Music Heritage Stage after she returned to the festival in 1988. She had spent almost her entire salary on it because she believed it was so important to record the oral histories of the musicians in clear, exact voices. Allison was a natural storyteller whose lyrical quality made those memories come alive.

She talked with enthusiasm, and with nostalgia that easily turned to tender tears. The theme somehow returned again and again to the life of the soul and how so many of her favorite musicians had died so young. Several times she used a metaphor of the spirit wearing down when life is hard, as if such sensitivity just couldn't last against such harsh obstacles. Now I know that Allison was speaking prophetically, for in just weeks she would be gone from us to be reunited with her heroes and soul mates: Robert Pete, Bukka, the Humphrey brothers, Mahalia, and Fess. She is playing triangle once again with Dewey Balfa and Canray Fontenot, as blissful as such an angel deserves to be.

CLARE BETH PIERSON

Jazz Fest
MEMORIES

Young Men Olympian Social & Pleasure Club, marching at the Fair Grounds, 1976. Alfred ("Bucket") Carter is the grand marshal.

Allison's Jazz Fest Memories

THE BEGINNING

It was 1969, the end of the psychedelic era; the Beatles White Album was popular and the Chicago Transit Authority was wondering if anybody really knew what time it was. I had been in New Orleans for two years, happily working for Dick Allen in the Jazz Archives at Tulane University. One day the phone rang, and the voice on the other end of the line asked, "May I speak to Dick Allen? This is George Wein."

"Oh," I answered. "You're the man who's going to be doing the jazz festival. Dick has asked me if I'd like to be involved, and I know you're looking for young people to help."

George's very next words were: "Yes, we're looking for young people who want to be *exploited*."

I said, "Well, great. I have a friend named Quint Davis who's a real expert on rhythm and blues and contemporary jazz, and I know a lot about traditional jazz and country blues. So, yeah, I'd love to meet with you."

Our first meeting was at Cafe du Monde, and over coffee and beignets I sort of "signed up." So did Quint. Now all we had to do was everything else that it would take to put the first New Orleans Jazz & Heritage Festival together. The next step was to go out and get the music.

OUT AND ABOUT

The music scene in New Orleans was mainly Bourbon Street and disco. To book the music for the first festival, we went to the only places where live music was really happening: the black clubs. We went to the Night Cap Lounge, on Louisiana Avenue, and the Off Limits, where Willie Tee and Earl Turbinton played. We had no contracts, just our voices and ourselves. We would go and hang out, drink a beer, dance, talk to people, and just be friends. That has always been one of the secrets of the success of the festival; from the beginning it has always been about people, not money or tremendous crowds or national acclaim but wonderful people whom I've always been proud to call my friends.

We did our fieldwork by telephone, and unfortunately I didn't have one. We would go to All Good's Restaurant across from Touro Infirmary and use their pay phone to make our calls. I remember calling Snooks Eaglin at his mother-in-law's house. Dick Allen had given us the number. Snooks was the first person we booked for the festival. At that time he was a street singer. He didn't play in any club, just for neighborhood groups and churches. Snooks played at the first festival and has played at every festival since. Another musician who came on board at the very beginning and has played every year since is Clancy ("Blues Boy") Lewis. He was at the Triangle Lounge in Gert Town, and he was fantastic.

At that time no one else was "out and about." Intergration laws had just been passed, and people like Allan and Sandra Jaffe were getting arrested for having black people in Preservation Hall. So here we were, two young people trying to put on a multiethnic music festival, and that had never been done before in the Deep South city of New Orleans.

On Sunday mornings we would listen to live church-radio broadcasts, and the shows would announce the concerts for the afternoon. One Sunday we heard that there was to be a program of gospel music at St. John's Institutional Baptist Church at four o'clock. Of course, we went and that afternoon met the Zion Harmonizers and Lois DeJean for the first time. They became part of the festival that day and have been part of it ever since. I fondly remember another Sunday when we visited a Sanctified church off of Airline Highway that Larry Borenstein had told us about. There we met Elder Ott and the Ott Family Singers. We became friends immediately. Elder Ott is on the Jazz Festival staff today, still working hard to make the Gospel Tent a wonderfully spiritual experience.

Quint and I soon realized that we had no white people. To remedy this we started reading posters around town. One in particular read Big Walker Bluegrass Jamboree. I called the number on the poster and said, "Hello. This is Allison Miner, calling from New Orleans. My friend and I are interested in coming to your festival."

"Oh, you're from New Orleans?" the man responded. "Would you be the judges of our talent show?" He had no idea that we were young kids, and we had no idea that Walker, Louisiana, was a hotbed of Ku Klux Klan activity. So we agreed to be the judges, and they treated us like royalty. There were Confederate flags everywhere, but nobody seemed to notice but us. The winner of the talent show was Hubert Davis and the Season Travelers. Hubert had played with Bill Monroe as a young man. The band members were all his family. We met the Meyers Brothers Bluegrass Band, and they were fabulous.

Another one of my favorite memories, one that I never want to forget, has to do with the sense of "family" that permeates the festival. I think it was the third year, and Hubert Davis had performed the same day as the Ott Family Singers. Hubert came to me and said, "You know, we've been in Nashville most of our lives, and we never played with black people before." Then he smiled so warmly and sincerely and said, "But we sure love the Ott family now, and we love your festival." The Ott family was standing right there, and they all smiled at each other and then started hugging each other. It's so amazing what the festival has done to change people's lives. It was happening to them right then and there, and we were all very thankful.

SHOWTIME

The first festival was held in Congo Square, which is now a part of Armstrong Park, on Rampart Street. There was a Gospel Tent and four other open stages. Some of the stages had no microphones. Fortunately, musicians like Babe Stovall and Brother Percy Randolph were so powerful that they didn't need mikes. They just sat out there on chairs and played and sang.

There was so much love at that festival. The visiting artists came on Greyhound buses and stayed at our house. There was no money in the budget for hotels. Great musicians like Bukka White, Big Joe Williams, and Robert Pete Williams stayed with us. They were such incredible musicians and such remarkable men that it was a privilege and a pleasure to have them. We were a family and we all loved each other.

From those early days, I'd like to think that my contribution has been maternal. I have always wanted to make sure the musicians were treated right, that they were fed and had an experience that they happily remembered. They were part of a festival that touched people's lives.

The city of New Orleans built the stages for us, but when it came time for the festival to begin, we realized that all we had were platforms. Joyce Wein and I went to Krauss and bought yards and yards of fabric. We decorated and waited. And waited. Nobody came. There were about three hundred musicians and volunteers and only about fifty people in the audience. We took a roll of tickets to the nearby public school and gave all the children tickets for that weekend. We told them to come and bring their parents. It was embarrassing that nobody came. Then when the music started, the people in the neighborhood just took pocketknives and slit the thin canvas fence that we had put up. We didn't even care; at least there were people.

Until that first festival I had never heard live Cajun music, only bad recordings. I'll never forget that first time hearing it in its authentic, traditional form. I was standing in Congo Square, and I heard a triangle, which has become my favorite instrument. You just have to have something special to play the triangle. When I heard it, I went flying across the square. I screamed, "It's real! It really exists!" I just couldn't believe it; it made me cry. It was so real and foreign that it was like going to another land.

Another music form that has been represented at the festival since the very beginning is Mardi Gras Indian music. One of my earliest mentors, photographer Jules Cahn, introduced me to jazz funerals, "second-line" processions, and Indian parades. He would drag me to every event that was going on, and we would film and photograph until I was exhausted. I'd say, "Jules, please. I'm starving. Can we get something to eat?"

Without even a glance my way he'd say, "Oh, Allison, don't be such a slave to your stomach!"

One night Jules and I went to Barrows and Sons Lounge. Jules had me holding the lights and the microphones while he was filming. When we got home, we listened to the tape and noticed Bo Dollis's voice for the first time, since we had been so busy while working at the lounge. Both of us said, "Who in the hell is that? What a voice! Listen to that guy!" Then we had to find him.

We got the phone number of a bar on Washington Avenue where Bo hung out. I called and asked if we could set up a meeting with him. Well, not only did we meet with him but with about thirty other Indians. When Quint and I walked into the meeting place, a bar on Dryades Street, they were all just standing there looking at us: two young white kids. We were children trying to describe the festival as best we could, and they said that they'd do it. I think we were all shocked, but they were a superb part of the festival. They paraded from Jackson Square to Congo Square, and it was really magnificent. The Wild Magnolias and the Golden Eagles have been at the festival from the very first one.

The festival was a labor of love. Quint and I didn't even get paid. George took us out to dinner at all of the finest restaurants in town. We loved every minute of what we were doing. We were committed to the music and knew that we were doing something worthwhile, something that counted, something that would be a lasting memorial to the people and the music that they were making. Seeing Mahalia Jackson was all the reward I could ever have wanted.

Mahalia Jackson simply appeared at the first festival. She was singing in a musical in town and heard about the festival. She came out and began singing with one of the brass bands. This gorgeous, unbelievably majestic soul sang "A Closer Walk." Next to Louis Armstrong, she is probably the greatest singer ever to come out of New Orleans. I was in awe of her! Everyone was.

THE SECOND YEAR

One of the most amazing performers at the second festival was Henry Roeland Byrd, a.k.a. Professor Longhair. Until the festival I had only heard of him through recordings of music and an interview that were on file at the archives. The sound of the interview was so bad. They must have been on a front porch with cars going by. Quint also had a recording of one of Fess's most renowned songs, "Big Chief." Even though the recording was poor, the talent on it was obvious.

When Byrd came out to the festival, he was carrying an aluminum folding chair for a woman who was supposed to be one of his managers. He referred to her as "Miss Terry." His suit was so shiny. It must have been pressed so many times that it practically wasn't there.

He wasn't performing anymore. He was working as a custodian, sweeping the floor at the One Stop Record Shop in the 1500 block of South Rampart Street. That day he got up on the stage with just a drummer, Edmund Kimbro. Snooks Eaglin was playing on another stage. Quint asked Snooks to come and perform on stage with Fess.

When the three of them started to play, the entire festival stopped and everyone came over to see and hear these great musicians. It was truly amazing, even in that very early stage of Fess's "comeback." He was definitely a presence, but he wasn't yet what he was to become. He was malnourished and run-down. He had had such a hard, hard time.

From that time on, we were Byrd's friends. He came to our house almost every day; he became part of our lives, Quint's and mine. Fess and I had a talkative relationship as only a man and woman who are close friends can have. He said I was a lot like his wife, Alice, who was also a Libra. They had been together since the 1930s. We became an extended family.

AND THE REST IS HISTORY

By the third festival we had moved to the Fair Grounds. This site was so large compared to Congo Square, and the festival was practically empty that year. We didn't have much staff and very few volunteers.

The Fair Grounds had no drainage system, and after one of the first days of the festival, it rained. Quint, Henry Hildebrand III, and I picked up all the garbage in the rain and slush at the end of the day. In those early days people brought their own drinks, and there were broken whiskey bottles everywhere. When I look at how the festival has changed over the years, I find it hard to believe.

I remember one night when, even though I was exhausted, I was so exhilarated that I ended up partying all night long at the Cornstalk Hotel in the French Quarter with the sound crew from Massachusetts. I got home early in the morning to find Robert Pete and Bukka in the kitchen. Both of them had on my aprons. Robert Pete was washing dishes and Bukka was sweeping the floor. They were shocked and scandalized that I had stayed out all night. Both of them asked, "Where have you been all night?" It was so funny to see them standing there in aprons, scolding me as though I were a naughty child.

Those men are still my heroes. They were not just ordinary men; they carried the oral history of a proud musical tradition. They led such hard lives, like Professor Longhair, who died at sixty-one. The soul gets worn down when you have such a difficult life. Robert Pete collected metal and resold it. He had been a sharecropper. Brother Percy Randolph was a junk collector who rode a bike around the city. He played harmonica and rub board. For all these men the festival gave them their identity. For the time each played on stage, he was somebody. When the festival was over, they went back to their hard lives. It never ceased to amaze me that they could sustain such joy and beauty in their music when they had such a difficult time with life. They did whatever they could the rest of the year to stay alive, like collecting scrap metals. Many of them had never been heard, nor ever would be were it not for the New Orleans Jazz & Heritage Festival. I am proud that I helped make that happen for many of them, and I'm very happy to know that music continues to be important in this city.

In New Orleans, people can hear music year round now because there is such a talent base. The festival helps support music and musicians.

JAZZ FEST MEMORIES

There is more music per square foot in New Orleans than in any other city in the world, and it's a hell of a lot of fun. It's our life! When I pass down St. Claude Avenue and see some boys and girls coming home from school holding their musical instruments, I get such a warm feeling. I think, oooh, they're continuing the tradition; they're doin' it.

When I first came to New Orleans from Daytona Beach, I thought I was going to take the city by storm. The truth is that the city took me by storm. I love New Orleans, and I'm glad that I've made a contribution to it. When I came as a kid, I hoped that I would. I never thought it would be such a wonderful people experience. Even when a stranger who had listened to one of my interviews says, "That was fantastic," it really means something to me. What I've done has changed people's lives. They come to hear the music and listen to the words of the great men and women who sing and tell the stories of life, and they go away transformed.

In the early days, I knew that the festival was more than the music. It was a family of hardworking people who gave their lives for what they believed. This fully functional family labored together and loved each other and put on the greatest musical festival in the world, in the only city where such a phenomenon could succeed so well because of its commitment to and support of music.

One of my latest memories is of George Wein at the piano, poised and ready to play. He looked and me and said, "This is for you, kid." He played "Thanks a Million."

Bill Russell playing violin with the New Orleans Ragtime Orchestra at the first Jazz Fest, 1970. Those of us who had the honor of knowing William Russell felt that he was a very saintly, self-sacrificing person. His American Music record label, started here in the forties, paved the way for the revival of interest in traditional jazz.

AT LEFT:
Fats Houston and Anderson Minor (holding the umbrella) in a crowded second line on the infield of the New Orleans Fair Grounds, 1973.

Louis Cottrell leading the Onward Brass Band, 1972. Cottrell was the president of the black musicians' union, Local No. 496 AFM, prior to its merging with the white No. 174 AFM. He began playing with the Young Tuxedo Orchestra at sixteen.

Multi-instrumentalist Rahsaan Roland Kirk sitting in with the Olympia Brass Band; Joe ("Red") Texadore, percussionist, in hat next to Kirk, 1973. I knew that Rahsaan had been to a jazz funeral a few days prior to this but was totally astounded to hear him be able to imitate Emmanuel Paul, sax player with the Olympia, so perfectly.

This is probably one of the most exciting moments I experienced at the fair (1973). Stevie Wonder finished his sound check and came out to sit in with the Meters. I was backstage as Stevie climbed the stairs to join them. His energy and beautiful smile were almost palpable. They played "Superstition" and the crowd went wild.

Sister Gertrude Morgan preaching from her tabernacle at the fair, 1973. Her megaphone is hanging from a string. Sister Gertrude participated in the festival from the beginning. She always insisted on a roof over her head to speak the Holy Word. Her paintings were dominated by Scriptures and angels.

Benny Spellman (1974), a consummate New Orleans entertainer whose biggest hits, "Fortuneteller" and "Lipstick Traces," were written and produced by Allen Toussaint.

The Meters: Art Neville, George Porter, Jr., and Joseph ("Zigaboo") Modeliste, 1974. The conga player in front is Alfred ("Uganda") Roberts.

Jewel ("Babe") Stovall, from Washington Parish, Louisiana, was one of the only country blues guitarists working in New Orleans at this time (1974). He played his National Steel guitar in Jackson Square through the sixties, made one album for Verve Records, and was with the festival from the first day in Congo Square.

The legendary Danny Barker grand marshaling a parade on the infield, with a plastic cigar and the right attitude, 1974

AT RIGHT:
Jeanette Carter on Autoharp performing traditional Appalachian folk songs, 1974. Her mother was Maybelle from the Original Carter Family.

Gary Brown on saxophone with Allen Toussaint on piano. This was Toussaint's first appearance in a Jazz Fest night concert; it took place on the SS *Admiral* on April 24, 1975.

A youthful Clifton Chenier, with John Hart on saxophone, 1976. Clifton's music defined contemporary zydeco. His repertoire was enormous and he was known for keeping his band playing up to four hours without a break.

AT RIGHT:
Joseph Pierre ("Monk") Boudreaux and John ("Quartermoon") Tobias in their Young Men Olympian finery, 1976. Both men masked as Golden Eagles and recorded with the Wild Magnolias Mardi Gras Indians.

The Jolly Bunch Social & Pleasure Club, 1975.

Charles, Cyril, Ivan, and Aaron Neville, 1977.

Cyril, Ivan, and Aaron Neville creating a sweet harmony, 1977.

Charles Neville with the Wild Tchoupitoulas Mardi Gras Indians, 1977.

George ("Big Chief Jolly") Landry of the Wild Tchoupitoulas and Percy ("Big Chief Pete") Lewis of the Black Eagles, 1977.

The Fairview Baptist Church Band (1977), which was started by Danny Barker at his neighborhood church. This really marked the resurgence of very young musicians putting bands together in hopes of getting work.

Ella Fitzgerald and Stevie Wonder at the Municipal Auditorium, 1977. This was another of those magical moments, when Stevie decided he wanted to join Ella on stage. He came out of the audience, and after they put their heads together for a moment, we heard "You Are the Sunshine of My Life."

37

The great "Bach of Rock," Henry Roeland Byrd, also known as Professor Longhair, 1977. From the first year he played the festival in 1971, Fess became the focal point of the event. He used to refer to the fair as "The Fiesta." I love this image because he is finishing a song by whipping his arm off the keyboard with one powerful, dramatic motion.

Ironing Board Sam, or Sammy Moore, with his invention, the ironing-board keyboard, 1977. I first met Sam at Mason's Motel, where Quint Davis and I went to hear him. He was working with a drummer who set his sticks on fire (yes, actually on fire) and after the gig Sam proudly showed us his fake-fur-lined Cadillac.

Bonnie Raitt, slide-guitar queen of contemporary blues pop, 1977.

The Meyers Brothers Bluegrass Band from Walker, Louisiana, 1977. This group played the fair for years after Quint and I heard them at the Walker Bluegrass Jamboree.

In the days before the festival was so terribly crowded, there used to be places to sit down and have a peaceful picnic (1978).

A young Norman Dixon with Young Men Olympian, 1978. Today Norman is the coordinator of all the brass bands and social aid and pleasure clubs that parade the infield.

One of the great voices ever to be heard from the Crescent City, Irving Lee Dorsey, 1978. Lee could make any song sound great (e.g., "Sittin' in La La Waitin' for My Ya Ya"). He worked extensively with Allen Toussaint, who wrote songs with Lee specifically in mind, such as "Lover of Love." Lee's biggest hits included "Working in a Coal Mine," "Ride Your Pony," and "Holy Cow," to name a few.

Coushatta Indian basket maker Lorena B. Langley, from Elton, Louisiana, 1978. Mrs. Langley was the first traditional-crafts person I contacted to be a part of the festival. She has a large family, including her daughter and grandsons who work with her to be the best basket makers among the Coushatta.

Exuma, from Cat Island in the Bahamas, brought his distinctive sounds to New Orleans for several years (1978).

Clifton Chenier and John Hart, 1978. Cleveland Chenier is in the background.

Clifton Chenier at a riverboat night concert, 1979

Eubie Blake on one of his many visits to our festival, 1979. Blake, a composer and pianist from Baltimore, was one of the great ragtime interpreters.

James Rivers, wailing on the saxophone (1979), is known as a great bagpipe improviser. Recently Rivers was chosen to appear in the film *The Bridges of Madison County.*

The Nevilles, featuring Jason, son of Aaron Neville, 1979.

Alvin Alcorn and Teddy Riley lead a second line through the fair, 1980.

Young Raymond Myles with his mother, "Sister" Christine Myles, in the Gospel Tent, 1980.

AT LEFT:
The Gentlemen of Leisure preparing to march, 1979.

The Mighty Rocks of Harmony jumping for joy in the Gospel Tent, 1980.

This is the one thing I eat every year without fail—it's the best (1980).

These two accordion players decided to serenade the people waiting in line for crawfish pie and filé gumbo, 1980. Look at those low prices.

Allen Toussaint playing guitar at one of the riverboat night concerts, 1980.

George Coleman ("Bongo Joe"), from San Antonio, Texas, had a memorial to Professor Longhair in front of his gazebo in 1980. Coleman played fifty-gallon oil drums with mallets made of rock-filled oil cans held together with silver tape. He sang in a kind of rap/calypso style and was a great whistler. He happened to be the first musician I ever had to pick up at the airport, in 1971, and his first request was to pick some mace and then go see the Mississippi River.

B. B. King and His Orchestra, working hard as always, 1980. Calvin Owens is the bandleader and trumpet player.

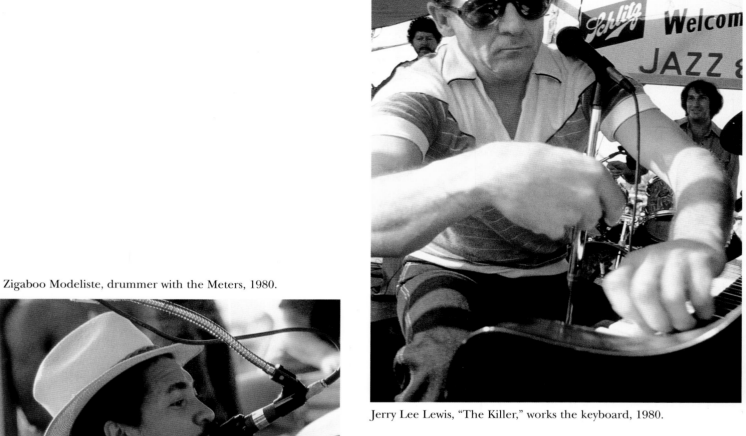

Jerry Lee Lewis, "The Killer," works the keyboard, 1980.

Zigaboo Modeliste, drummer with the Meters, 1980.

Clarence ("Frogman") Henry wows the crowd with his classic hit, "I Ain't Got a Home," 1980.

Fats Domino surrounded by admirers, 1980.

Fats Domino with Dave Bartholomew, 1980.

The magnificent Dorothy Donegan, 1981. Once a child prodigy in classical music, Dorothy has one of the most powerful piano styles in jazz.

AT LEFT:
Dave Bartholomew, the crowd pleaser and Fats Domino's bandleader and arranger, with Lee Allen on saxophone, 1980. Fats was fortunate to have Dave as his arranger for his countless hits produced in the fifties. The first 45 I ever played over and over, at age eight, was the *B* side of "Blueberry Hill," "Honey Chile."

Hugh Masekela on one of his many visits to the festival, 1981. Originally from South Africa, Masekela spent many years in exile during the harsh years of repression in his country. He became well known in America for his song "Grazing in the Grass."

The Golden Eagles on the old "Fess Stage," 1981

The front line of the Johnny Wiggs Camellia Band: Frank Demond (trombone), Clive Wilson (trumpet), Johnny Wiggs (cornet), and Raymond Burke (clarinet), 1981.

AT LEFT:
Some of the popular food selections at the fair, 1981. Notice the tie-dye bunting.

One of my childhood heroes, Chuck Berry, 1981. Chuck Berry and Little Richard, in my opinion, wrote the definitive songs of rock and roll.

Junior Walker at the Theatre of the Performing Arts in Armstrong Park, 1981.

Clifton Chenier and friend take in the fair, 1981.

Clifton observing an impromptu set by Marc and Ann Savoy in Marc's booth in the crafts area, 1981. Also in the audience are Cleveland Chenier and Chris Strachwitz of Arhoolie Records.

Floyd Anckle leads the Majestic Brass Band and second-line followers on the infield, 1981.

Alice Byrd's booth at the festival, 1981. Michael P. Smith created a poster that he donated to Professor Longhair's widow to assist her financially after her husband's death. Collectors enjoyed getting Alice to autograph the poster and visiting with her. Note photographer Jules Cahn in the foreground.

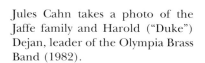

Jules Cahn takes a photo of the Jaffe family and Harold ("Duke") Dejan, leader of the Olympia Brass Band (1982).

The Buckjumpers and Young Men Olympian social and pleasure clubs parade at the Fair Grounds, 1982.

Bessie Griffin in the Gospel Tent, 1982.

AT LEFT:
Offstage drummers attract an audience, 1982. Jam sessions are common in the infield.

Smokin' Dragon from the Krewe of Clones visits the festival, 1982.

Chuck Berry flying, 1982.

Chuck Berry and his lovely daughter, Ingrid, 1982.

AT LEFT:
Double-Dutch jumpers find a spot on the asphalt to draw some attention to their talents, 1982.

The Roman Candy man, 1982. A fixture in our community, this wagon has carried three generations of family proprietors. The current "candy man" is Ron Kottemann. The Neapolitan flavored taffy is a taste from the past.

Crowd, 1982.

Bassist Walter Payton conducts his orchestra from McDonogh No. 15 School in the French Quarter, 1982.

Ed Volker and the Radiators get down with their "Fishhead" sound, 1982. Ed is a provocative and prolific songwriter who has devoted his life to creating a distinct music from New Orleans.

The one and only James Black on drums, with Jim Singleton on bass and David Torkanowsky in the background on piano, in the Jazz Tent, 1982.

The greatest New Orleans recording engineer of all time, Cosimo Matassa. Matassa owned several studios during the fifties, sixties, and seventies where the biggest New Orleans hits were made. Here he is running the sound board at the Jazz Tent, 1983.

The good old days, when ice chests at the Jazz Fest were still legal, 1983.

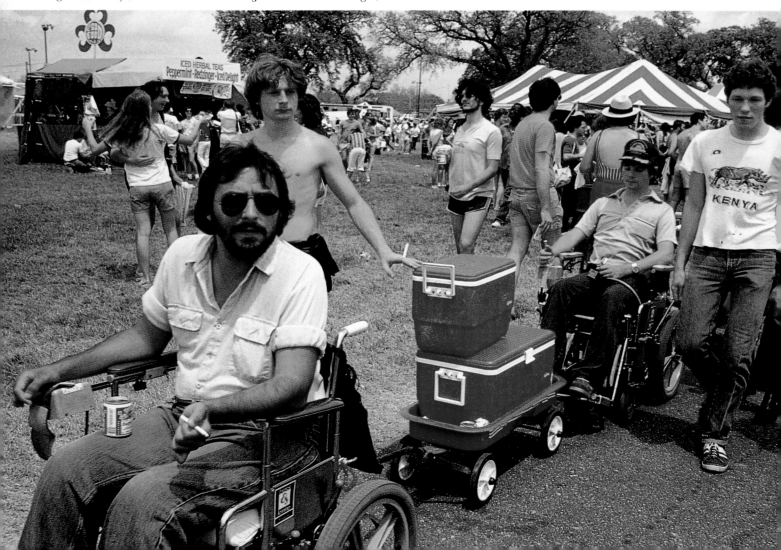

Gospel Inspirations of Kenner, Louisiana, 1983.

Sister Katie Bell, 1983. Her family was a strong evangelical influence in the Avondale area.

Jam in the crafts area, 1983.

Jim Jenkins, blacksmith, fires up his tools for a demonstration in the crafts area, 1984.

Bobby Marchan, well-known emcee and entertainer, with Elliot Snellings, attorney, photographer, and festival volunteer, 1984.

The "Shakespeare of the Blues,"
great songwriter and bassist Willie
Dixon, 1984.

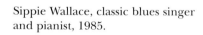

Sippie Wallace, classic blues singer
and pianist, 1985.

Staff of the festival: Quint Davis, Nancy Ochsenschlager, Laura Laughlin, Robert Leslie Jones, Kelly Sullivan, and Joanne Schmidt, 1985.

White Eagle Mardi Gras Indians, with Big Chief Jake Millon on lead vocals, 1985.

Ernest ("Doc") Paulin on trumpet with some sidemen and family members, including young son Roderick on saxophone, 1985. Paulin, in his early seventies here, is originally from Wallace, Louisiana. His grandfather was a French-speaking accordion player.

Willie Humphrey, older brother of Percy (1985). Willie had one of the sweetest tones of anyone who played traditional New Orleans jazz.

Trumpeter and bandleader Percy Humphrey, 1985. Humphrey last performed at the Jazz Festival in 1995, singing "When the Saints Go Marching In" with his band in the Economy Hall tent. As leader of the Eureka Jazz Band and star of the touring Preservation Hall Jazz Band, Humphrey had a long career working with his two brothers, Willie, clarinet, and Earl, trombone.

Benny Spellman with Lee Allen and Alvin ("Red") Tyler on saxophones, 1985.

Lionel Batiste of the Treme Sports marching club "cools it" at the Fair Grounds, 1985.

Stevie Ray Vaughan in full regalia hanging out backstage, 1986.

Earl King, Stevie Ray Vaughan, and Dave Bartholomew getting to know one another, 1986.

The magnificent, fiery Betty Carter in the Jazz Tent, 1986.

Bo Dollis and the Wild Magnolias, 1986.

The Young Tuxedo Brass Band lines up for a parade in the infield, 1986.

Junkanoos bringing a colorful parade to the festival, 1986. These costumes, which are made of paper-mache, are used in Christmas mumming in former British colonial islands, including the Bahamas.

AT RIGHT:
Katie Webster, from Lake Charles, Louisiana, 1988. Katie, one of the rare female blues-piano players, has a unique piano and vocal style.

The Zion Harmonizers: Nolan Washington, Alvin Thomas, Howard Bowie, Joseph Warrick, Sherman Washington, and Willie Williams, 1987. This was one of the first groups booked for the festival. The leader, Sherman Washington, is our gospel coordinator.

Dennis McGee, a master of the Cajun fiddle, 1988. Along with his brother-in-law, Sady Courville, Dennis came to New Orleans in the late twenties to record classic fiddle duets on 78s. A farmer and part-time musician, Dennis became an icon in later years, playing festivals around the country.

Irvin J. Perez, woodcarver from St. Bernard, Louisiana, 1989. Irvin won the National Folk Heritage Award in 1991. He is an accomplished singer, carrying on the tradition of his Isleño ancestors from the Canary Islands who sang a-cappella songs known as décimas.

Miles Davis, 1989.

Wynton Marsalis, 1989.

Drummer Herlin Riley with the Wynton Marsalis big band, 1989. Herlin is the grandson of Deacon Frank Lastie, who played drums with Louis Armstrong when Satchmo was still in New Orleans; the son of Betty Ann Lastie; and the nephew of David, Walter, and Melvin Lastie—all legendary New Orleans musicians.

Tent City is no longer allowed at the festival (1989). It started small and became a major problem for pedestrian traffic. But is was fun while it lasted.

AT LEFT:
Wynton Marsalis's sidemen at the
River Tent the night before it blew
down, 1989.

Champion Jack Dupree, pianist, singer, composer, and extraordinary human being, 1990. Jack returned to New Orleans for the first time in forty years to play the festival and see family. His spirit was irrepressible. Jack was a former kosher cook, boxer, and world traveler who in recent years worked throughout Europe, with Hannover, Germany as his home base. I had the pleasure of a private breakfast interview with him after his first visit home. We talked about the days we spent working with Professor Longhair. I decided to take him and the band to the airport following breakfast. Along I-10 Jack looked out at the apartment complexes in Kenner and commented disparagingly, "They look like bird cages."

Champion Jack Dupree in his homemade Indian finery, 1991. As a youth, Jack had masked as a member of the Yellow Pocahontas Mardi Gras Indians, and among his pastimes were painting, creating beautiful beadwork, and decorating moccasins.

John Mayall (1991), father of the British blues scene. I had a great interview with Mayall at the festival in 1995. He has made so many recordings in his career, but the most recent featured a great song written by guitarist Sonny Landreth, "Congo Square."

AT LEFT:
Rockin Tabby Thomas (1991), musician and proprietor of Tabby's Blues Box, a club that has single-handedly kept the blues thriving in Baton Rouge. Tabby is the father of Chris Thomas.

John Mooney and Ed Bradley schmooze and groove backstage, 1991.

93

Art Neville at the keys, 1991. From the early days of the Hawkettes and "Mardi Gras Mambo," Neville has distinguished himself as a leader in the New Orleans music scene. He is a quiet, mature man who works doubly hard by keeping up responsibility with the Funky Meters as well as the Neville Brothers.

AT RIGHT:
GARIFUNA, a folklore ensemble from Belize, performs a voodoo ceremony, 1991.

Miles Davis, 1991. This was his last Jazz Fest appearance, as he died later that year.

Kristin ("KiKi") Armstrong, a snake dancer with the Dr. John ensemble, prepares to bring her snake to center stage, 1992.

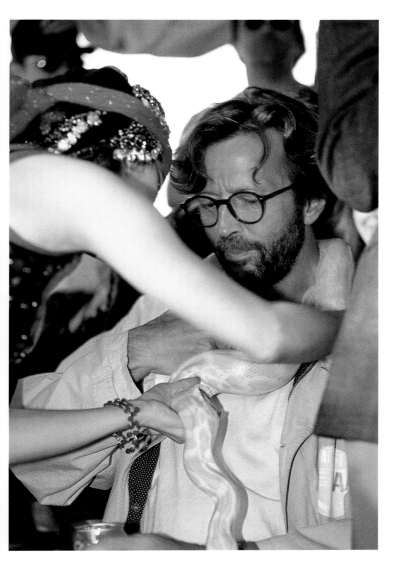

Kiki wraps Eric Clapton backstage.

Eric warms up to the snake.

AT LEFT:
Kiki center stage with Dr. John, with
Smiley Ricks on congas.

VOODOO
PRIESTESS
AVA KAY JONES

PSYCHIC · READINGS
PRIVATE CONSULTATIONS
GRIS-GRIS BAGS
VOODOO DOLLS
POTIONS
HELP BRING YOU
LOVE, PEACE & PROSPERITY

WE FOCUS ONLY

AT LEFT:
Ava Kay Jones, 1992. Now how many other festivals feature a voodoo booth? Ava Kay was a parent volunteer at McDonogh No. 15 School in the Quarter when my children were attending. During the school's Spring Fundraising Festival, she would perform her snake dance as part of the entertainment.

LOWER LEFT
Parker Dinkins working his remote audio station behind the Music Heritage Stage, 1992. Parker has been affiliated with the festival for a number of years as fair director and legal counsel.

Wayne Bennett and Willie Lockett, 1992. Guitarist Bennett was a fixture at Bobby ("Blue") Bland sessions.

Raymond Anthony Myles, keyboard player, vocalist, and choir director, 1992.

Davell Crawford, an up-and-coming pianist, singer, and choir director, 1992. Davell is the grandson of Sugar Boy Crawford. I had the pleasure of booking Davell on piano night at Tipitina's after hearing him at the New Orleans Center for Creative Arts high school (NOCCA).

Edwin ("Eddie Bo") Bocage putting down his licks, 1992. Eddie Bo is an accomplished songwriter, pianist, singer, arranger, and all-around entertainer. Bocage released nearly as many 45s as Fats Domino. Recently he has traveled internationally and enjoyed much delayed recognition.

Allison Miner interviewing Ellis Marsalis on the Music Heritage Stage in the paddock area, 1992.

Terrance Simien of Mallet, Louisiana, 1992. Simien had his first formal gig at the 1984 World's Fair Folk Life Pavilion in New Orleans. He has developed a unique style of zydeco that incorporates New Orleans rhythm and blues. His first 45, "You Used to Call Me," featured Paul Simon on background vocals.

Wayne Toups (1992) from Crowley, Louisiana, is the powerhouse of contemporary Cajun and zydeco. He is also a fine interpreter of the traditional repertoires.

Amasa Miller (1992), in his snake-festooned top hat, is a versatile keyboard player. He is a regular with Charmaine Neville's band.

Alton Rubin (Rockin' Dopsie) with Allison Miner backstage, 1992.

Gladys Knight, 1992.

Gladys Knight, glamorous and energized by the audience, 1992.

AT LEFT:
Soul singer Ann Peebles of Memphis visits the Fair Grounds in 1992 to promote a new recording of her classic hit, "I Can't Stand the Rain."

105

Tattoo art is always displayed and appreciated at the Jazz Fest (1992).

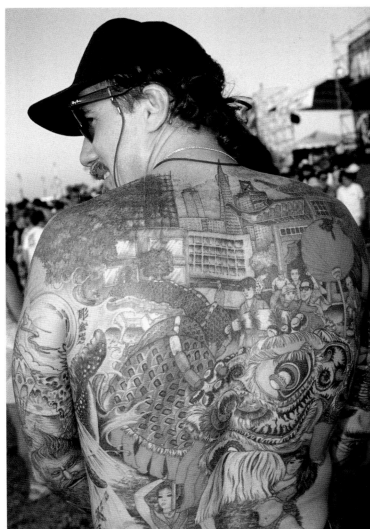

AT LEFT:
Johnny Winter, 1992

107

Tom Landry, Wild Magnolias Mardi Gras Indians, 1992.

AT LEFT:
Moa and the Moa Hunters, 1992.
Moas are extinct birds formerly
from New Zealand.

Dolls made by Lorraine Gendron,
1992.

Narvin Kimball, master of traditional jazz banjo, 1992. Mr. Kimball has played with the Preservation Hall Jazz Band for years. He began his career in the twenties with Papa Celestine's Original Tuxedo Orchestra.

Jeanette Kimball, niece of Isadore ("Tuts") Washington and former wife of Narvin Kimball, 1993. Jeanette is one of the rare women who works regularly with traditional jazz bands. In the background is trumpeter Clive Wilson.

Nelli Lutcher (1993), pianist and singer from Lake Charles, Louisiana, played with Bunk Johnson at age fifteen. After touring for many years, she settled in Los Angeles.

Nathan Williams and the Zydeco Cha Chas, 1993.

AT LEFT:
Moss Man Steve Nico gives a rare sax performance, 1993. He is a member of the audience rather than a paid participant.

"Deacon John" Moore (1993), master guitarist and singer, has been thrilling festival goers since the beginning with his myriad styles and vast experience. He is a real New Orleans treasure.

AT RIGHT:
John Mooney all dressed up and ready to get down, 1993.

Bob Dylan, 1993.

AT LEFT:
John Campbell at his last performance at our festival, 1993.

Instrument makers in the Traditional Folklife Village, 1993.

A crafts display of instrumental art, 1993.

AT RIGHT:
Lionel Key of Baton Rouge making "Uncle Bill's Filé," 1993. The family has made this product since 1904.

AT LEFT:
D. L. Menard of Erath, Louisiana, sometimes referred to as "The Cajun Hank Williams" (1993). Menard is the composer of the Cajun standard "The Back Door." He is also a chair builder when he is not touring as an ambassador of Cajun music.

Canadian producer/musician Daniel Lanois, 1993. Lanois produced the Neville Brothers' great album *Yellow Moon*, as well as recordings for U2 and Peter Gabriel.

Carlos Santana, 1993.

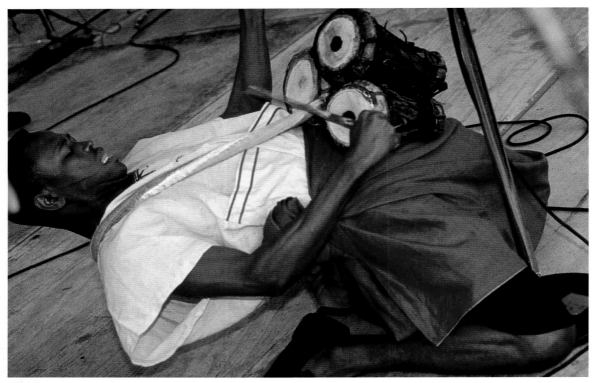

African musician Adewalye Ayuba-Fugi, 1993.

Larry Bannock, big chief, Golden Star Hunters, 1993.

Rain never stops the fun (1993).

A parade on Canal Street opened the twenty-fifth Jazz Fest, 1994. This is RAM of Haiti.

Twenty-fifth-anniversary parade, 1994.

Soul Rebels on Canal Street, 1994.

Better Boys Social & Pleasure Club, led by Wardell Lewis at the Fair Grounds, 1994.

The Monogram Hunters, from downtown, take the infield, 1994. This is "Wild Man" Demond.

Mardi Gras Indians from uptown take the infield too, 1994. This is Thomas ("Bo") Dean.

Bahamian Junkanoos, 1994.

Ali Farka Toure's band at the Fair Grounds' Congo Square, 1994.

Davell Crawford, 1994.

Crafts at Congo Square, 1994.

Traditional Native Americans dancing in the folk area, 1994.

Many Nations drummers, 1994.

AT LEFT:
One of the Many Nations dancers, 1994.

Willie Nelson, 1994.

Anders Osborne, a Swedish guitarist who is finding success in New Orleans, 1994.

The great B. B. King, "the dynamic gentleman of the blues," with his guitar, Lucille, 1994. This master of the blues guitar was born in Mississippi.

Beau Jocque, zydeco star (1994).

Dr. John, "The Night Tripper,"
1994.

135

Charles Brown, Texas pianist and vocalist par excellence, 1994.

AT RIGHT:
Solomon Burke with his son Haile
Selassie Burke, 1994.

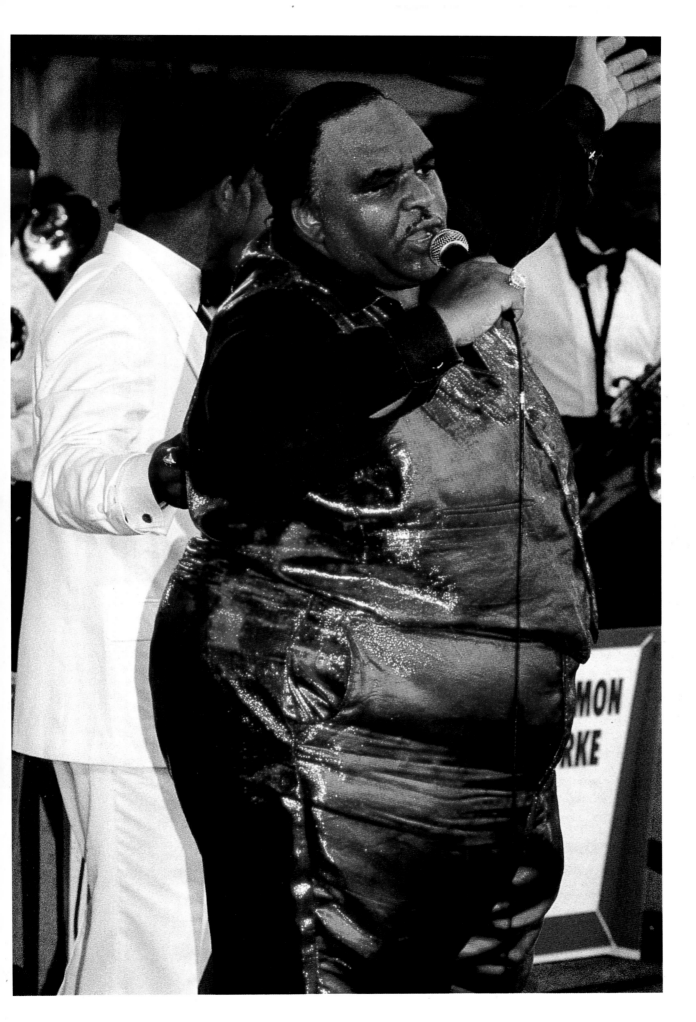

Tito Puente and Horace Silver meet backstage in the Jazz Tent, 1994.

AT LEFT:
Aretha Franklin wails at the twenty-fifth anniversary of the festival, 1994.

Jimmy Smith, 1994.

Adolphus Anthony ("Doc") Cheatham, 1995. The trumpeter and vocalist was born in 1905, in Nashville. Throughout a long and illustrious career, Doc played with nearly everyone, including Cab Calloway and the McKinney Cotton Pickers.

Leslie Smith, daughter of Michael P. Smith, 1994. Leslie is reviving her singing career, now that her babies are growing up. A fetching and provocative singer, she has worked predominantly with jazz sidemen.

Shannon Powell, one of New Orleans' most versatile drummers (1995). He was taught by the late jazz drummer James Black and toured extensively with Harry Connick, Jr.

AT LEFT:
Jim Singleton, bassist with the jazz group Astral Project and everyone else in town (1995).

David Torkanowsky on accordion, 1995. "Tork" is best known as Astral Project's piano genius.

143

Walter Mouton of Scott, Louisiana, 1995. Multi-instrumentalist Mouton is one of the rare Cajun musicians to develop his own unique style, often using steel guitar in his bands. The overall effect is a kind of Texas-swing/Cajun-contemporary sound.

Georgie and Allen Manuel, Cajun Mardi Gras screen-mask makers of Mamou, Louisiana, 1995.

Magnolia Sisters: Lisa McCauley, Ann Savoy, Jane Vidrine, Tina Piliove, and Allison Miner, 1995.

Uptowners Hobo Clowns Social Aid and Pleasure Club celebrate another Jazz Fest, 1995. Joe Bernard (in yellow shirt) has been a fixture in the local marching-club scene for some time as a grand marshal. This club is the most important extended-family masking group at Mardi Gras and the Jazz Fest.

Al Morris, big chief of the Northside Skull & Bone gang, in the grand-stand presentation area for traditional African-American culture, 1995.

Original Gentlemen Steppers marching club, 1995.

Zydeco star Furnest Arcenaux, 1995.

Rosie Ledet, Louisiana beauty and zydeco princess (1995).

Irma Thomas, Soul Queen of New Orleans (1995).

Gladys Knight, 1995.

Inez Andrews, from Birmingham, Alabama, one of the most powerful voices in all of gospel (1995). Her big hit in the seventies was "My Lord, You Don't Have to Move a Mountain."

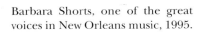

Barbara Shorts, one of the great voices in New Orleans music, 1995.

Leigh Harris, also known as Li'l Queenie (1995).

Eddie Volker of the Radiators, 1995.

The subdudes: Johnny Allen (bass), John Magnie (accordion), Steve Amadee (percussion), Tommy Malone (guitar), and Jason in the background (road manager), 1995.

Sonny Landreth, slide-guitar master, songwriter, and singer from Lafayette, Louisiana (1995).

Funk-blues guitarist Coco Robicheaux, 1995. One of his most well known accomplishments as a sculptor is the bust of Professor Longhair at Tipitina's.

George Wein and Quint Davis, the men who make it all happen (1995).

Henry Grey, 1995. Originally from Louisiana, Henry lived in Chicago for many years, where he worked with such blues masters as Muddy Waters.

Ray Charles, 1995.

Zigaboo Modeliste, original Meter, 1995.

Leo Nocentelli, original Meter, 1995.

Louise and Irvin J. Perez, with his prized woodcarvings, 1995.

Kissers: Bill and Vickie Sadin, 1995. People get married at the festival now. It could be called the most romantic event on earth!

Index